From the Books of
Presented by
Connor Beahm

COLOSSAL FOSSILS

COLOSSAL FOSSILS

DINOSAUR RIDDLES

Compiled by Charles Keller

Illustrated by Leonard Kessler

Simon and Schuster Books for Young Readers
Published by Simon & Schuster Inc., New York

Text copyright © 1987 by Charles Keller
Illustrations copyright © 1987 by Leonard Kessler
All rights reserved including the right of
reproduction in whole or in part in any form.
Published by Simon and Schuster Books for Young Readers
A Division of Simon & Schuster Inc.
Simon & Schuster Building
Rockefeller Center
1230 Avenue of the Americas
New York, NY 10020

10 9 8 7 6 5 4 3

Simon and Schuster Books for Young Readers
is a trademark of Simon & Schuster Inc.
Manufactured in the United States of America

Library of Congress Cataloging-in-Publication Data
Keller, Charles.
Colossal fossils.
SUMMARY: A collection of humorous riddles involving dinosaurs.
[1. Riddles.   2. Dinosaurs—Wit and humor]
I. Kessler, Leonard P., 1920–   ill.   II. Title.
PN6371.5.K383   1987   818'.5402   86-22656
ISBN 0-671-66532-4

For Nicole and Leigh

What was the fastest dinosaur called?
The prontosaurus.

What's as big as a dinosaur but doesn't weigh
anything?
His shadow.

What do you do with a blue dinosaur?
Cheer him up.

What did they call a dinosaur that was five feet tall?
Shortie.

What does a dinosaur do when it breaks a toe?
Gives up ballet dancing.

How can you tell a dinosaur from a peanut?
Try lifting it. If you can't, it's probably a dinosaur.
(But it might be a heavy peanut.)

What do you get when you cross a vampire and a
dinosaur?
A dinosaur that sleeps in the biggest coffin you ever
saw.

When a dinosaur gets old, what does it wear?
Out.

What's gray and powdery?
Instant dinosaur.

What's faster than a speeding bullet and eats tall buildings in a single bite?
Super Dinosaur.

What's brown on the outside and gray on the inside?
A chocolate-covered dinosaur.

Why did the dinosaur paint his toenails different colors?
So he could hide in the jelly bean jar.

Why did the caveman give up dinosaur hunting?
He got tired of carrying the decoys around.

What do you get when a dinosaur steps on your foot?
An anklosaurus.

What has 24 legs and goes crunch, crunch, crunch?
Six dinosaurs eating potato chips.

What do you do with a green dinosaur?
Wait until it ripens.

Which dinosaurs didn't get cavities?
The ones who brushed their teeth.

If you were walking in the jungle and saw a dinosaur, what time would it be?
Time to run.

What's the best way to talk to dinosaurs?
Long distance.

What's red, has a long neck, and hates to be touched?
A dinosaur with sunburn.

Why didn't dinosaurs play tennis?
Because there weren't any tennis shoes large enough.

Why did dinosaurs have such long necks?
Because their heads were so far from their bodies.

Why did the dinosaur cross the road?
It was the chicken's day off.

What has four wheels and a long neck?
A dinosaur on a skateboard.

How did dentists look at dinosaurs' teeth?
Very carefully.

How did the caveman know the dinosaur was in the shower with him?
He couldn't get the curtain closed.

Why did dinosaurs wear sneakers?
To creep up on mice.

Why did dinosaurs have wrinkled knees?
From playing marbles.

What do you get when you cross a dinosaur with a German shepherd?
A watchdog for the tenth floor.

What would you get if Batman and Robin were run over by a herd of stampeding dinosaurs?
Flatman and Ribbon.

What's worse than seeing a dinosaur's head in the jungle?
Seeing its tonsils.

What do you get when you cross a dinosaur with a cow?
I don't know, but you have to stand on a ladder to milk it.

Would you rather have a dinosaur attack you or a lion?
I'd rather have the dinosaur attack the lion.

How did the cavemen get fur from dinosaurs?
They ran in the opposite direction.

Why did dinosaurs have flat ears?
From wearing their cowboy hats too tight.

How did the caveman know a dinosaur was in his cave?
By the pajamas in the closet.

Why were dinosaurs big, gray, and wrinkled?
Because if they were small, white, and smooth, we'd think they were aspirins.

What weighs five tons, stores nuts for the winter, and climbs trees?
A dinosaur that thinks it's a squirrel.

What do you get when you cross a termite with a dinosaur?
A bug that eats the Empire State Building for breakfast.

How do you make a dinosaur stew?
Keep it waiting for a long time.

Why did the caveman have a dinosaur for a pet?
His wife was allergic to cats.

What's gray and goes up and down?
A dinosaur elevator operator.

How do we know dinosaurs were intelligent?
They were the highest form of animal life.

What did the baby dinosaur want for Christmas?
A toyrannosaurus.

What's red and white on the outside and gray on the inside?
Campbell's cream of dinosaur soup.

What would you get if you crossed a dinosaur with a mouse?
A mighty mouse.

What kind of tiles did dinosaurs put on their floors?
Rep-tiles.

Why didn't anyone want to sleep next to the father dinosaur?
He was a brontosnorus.

How did the caveman know a dinosaur was under his bed?
He banged his head on the ceiling.

What organization did the cavemen have for boys?
The Club Scouts.

What do you get when you cross a pigeon with a prehistoric creature?
A pigeon-toed dinosaur.

Why did dinosaurs have pointed tails?
From standing too close to the pencil sharpener.

What did the banana do when it saw the dinosaur?
The banana split.

What do you get when you cross a dinosaur with a snail?
The world's slowest dinosaur.

How are dinosaurs and bluebirds alike?
They both have wings, except for the dinosaurs.

What did the caveman say when he saw the dinosaur wearing sunglasses?
Nothing. He didn't recognize it.

Why don't they let dinosaurs drive cars?
Because there were too many tyrannosaurus wrecks.

What do you get when you cross a dinosaur with a pig?
The world's largest pork chops.

Why did dinosaurs jump across rivers?
So they wouldn't step on the fish.

What's the best way to get something out from under a dinosaur?
Wait for him to go away.

Why did dinosaurs live in the jungle?
They were too big to live in birdhouses.

What do you get when you cross a wild horse with a dinosaur?
A bronco-saurus.

Did dinosaurs get sore throats when they got wet feet?
Yes, but not until a week later.

What do you get if a dinosaur walks through a potato field?
Mashed potatoes.

What do you get when you cross a dinosaur with a spider?
I don't know, but when it crawls on your ceiling, the roof collapses.

Why were dinosaurs wrinkled?
Did you ever try to iron one?

What's red, blue, orange, and green?
A plaid dinosaur.

Why did dinosaurs have two front legs?
So they could turn the knobs on their tv's.

What's gray and plays trick-or-treat?
The Halloween dinosaur.

What did dinosaurs have that nobody else had?
Baby dinosaurs.

What do you get when you cross a dinosaur with a
kangaroo?
Leaping lizards.

What do you get when you cross a dinosaur with a
Venus flytrap?
A plant that eats elephants.

What do you say to a dinosaur to get him to hurry?
"Shake a legasaurus."

How does a dinosaur get into a tree?
He hides in an acorn and waits for a squirrel to carry him up.

What do you get when a dinosaur carries an elephant across the street?
A tired dinosaur.

Why didn't dinosaurs buy ten-speed bikes?
They couldn't use hand brakes.

What's gray and lives at the North Pole?
A lost dinosaur.

What always follows a dinosaur?
Its tail.

What do you call a petrified dinosaur?
A colossal fossil.

What do you get when you cross a dinosaur with an owl?
A creature that scares people but doesn't give a hoot.

What goes-clomp-clomp-clomp-thump, clomp-clomp-clomp-thump?
A dinosaur with a wooden leg.

What's more earth-shattering than an elephant
playing hopscotch?
Two dinosaurs playing leapfrog.

How do we know the cavemen played golf?
They always walked around with clubs in their hands.

What do you get when you cross a dinosaur and a mosquito?
I don't know, but if it bites you, you're in real trouble.

What do you get when you cross a dinosaur with a light bulb?
A walking street light.

What's gray and carries a basket of eggs?
The Easter dinosaur.

How much does a psychiatrist charge a dinosaur?
Fifty dollars for the visit and $500 for the couch.

Why did the dinosaur wear a red T-shirt?
His green one was in the wash.

What do you get when you cross a dinosaur with a cat?
A town without dogs.

What's the difference between a dinosaur and a
peanut butter sandwich?
A dinosaur doesn't stick to the roof of your mouth.

How can you tell the weight of a dinosaur?
By his scales.

Why didn't the cavemen walk through the jungle on Saturdays?
That's when the dinosaurs took their parachute lessons.

What do you get when you cross a dinosaur with a lawn mower?
A tree trimmer.

What's the difference between a tiny dinosaur and a large mouse?
About 10,000 pounds.

How did the cavemen make a dinosaur float?
They took two scoops of ice cream, some root beer, and a dinosaur.

Why did dinosaurs have big feet?
So they wouldn't slip in the bathtub.

How did the dinosaur get down from the tree?
He climbed on a leaf and waited for autumn.

Why did dinosaurs lie on their backs with their feet in the air?
To trip birds.

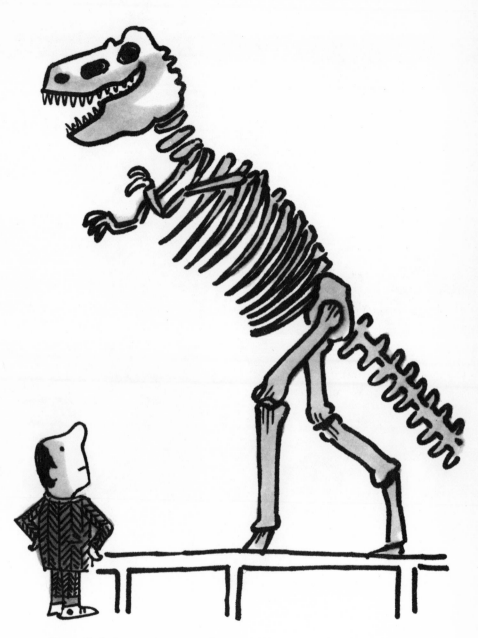

What did dinosaurs eat?
Judging by the ones in the museum, they didn't eat
anything.

How do you know when a dinosaur is about to charge?
He takes out his credit card.

What did the angry scientist say to the dinosaur fossil?
"I've got a bone to pick with you."

What weighs five tons and has four eyes, two noses, and four ears?
A dinosaur looking in a mirror.

What newspaper did the cavemen read?
The Prehistoric Times.

Why didn't dinosaurs sing?
They didn't want to be mistaken for birds.

Why were some dinosaurs vegetarians?
They couldn't afford 200 pounds of meat every day.

Could dinosaurs see in the dark?
Yes, but they had trouble holding the flashlight.

What did the dinosaur say when she couldn't find her eggs?
"I must have miss-laid them."

Why didn't the caveman tease the brontosaurus?
Because it made the dino-sore.

What's large and gray and bumps into submarines?
A dinosaur scuba diver.

What do you give a brontosaurus for his birthday?
A very, very long necktie.

What do you get when you cross a dinosaur with a ballerina?
Big holes in the floor.

How did dinosaurs move rocks?
With dino-might.

What did dinosaurs use to repair their homes?
Dino-saws and rep-tools.

How can you tell a baby dinosaur from a grown-up one?
The baby wears little booties.

Why did the dinosaur wear ripple-soled shoes?
To give the ants a fifty-fifty chance.

Why did the caveman play with the dinosaur?
It was tons of fun.

What did the scientist say when he found the dinosaur bones?
"I really dig this."

Why didn't dinosaurs laugh?
With all these terrible dinosaur jokes going around,
how could they?

ABOUT THE AUTHOR

Charles Keller is a popular author of humorous books for young people. His thirty-three previous books for Prentice-Hall include *Count Draculations! Monster Riddles, Waiter, There's A Fly in My Soup: Restaurant Jokes,* and *What's Up, Doc? Doctor and Dentist Jokes,* which is also illustrated by Leonard Kessler. Humor and folklore have always fascinated Mr. Keller, who also writes the syndicated newspaper column "Corn on the Cob." A native New Yorker, he now makes his home in Union City, New Jersey.

ABOUT THE ARTIST

Leonard Kessler is a renowned author and illustrator with nearly 200 books to his credit. Among them is Charles Keller's collection *What's Up, Doc? Doctor and Dentist Jokes* for which he did the very funny pictures. Mr. Kessler says he has been writing and drawing since he discovered colored pencils and paint at the age of six. He lives with his wife Ethel in New City, New York.